HUSKINGS, QUILTINGS, AND BARN RAISINGS

HUSKINGS, QUILTINGS, AND BARN RAISINGS

Work-Play Parties in Early America

Victoria Sherrow
Illustrations by Laura LoTurco

WALKER AND COMPANY
NEW YORK

First published in the United States of America in 1992
by Walker Publishing Company, Inc.

Published simultaneously in Canada by Thomas Allen & Son
Canada, Limited, Markham, Ontario

Library of Congress Cataloging-in-Publication Data
Sherrow, Victoria.
    Huskings, quiltings, and barn raisings: work-play parties in early
America / by Victoria Sherrow.
        p.   cm.
    Includes bibliographical references and index.
    Summary: Surveys the history of husking bees, barn raisings,
soap boilings, and other American work-play parties, in which
people in colonial and pioneer days came together to help one
another while having fun.
    ISBN 0-8027-8186-1. —ISBN 0-8027-8188-8 (reinforced)
    1. United States—Social life and customs—Colonial period, ca.
1600–1775—Juvenile literature. 2. United States—Social life and
customs—1783–1865—Juvenile literature. 3. Handicraft—United
States—History—Juvenile literature. [1. United States—Social
life and customs—Colonial period, ca. 1600–1775. 2. United
States—Social life and customs—1783–1865.] I. Title.
E162.S55   1992
973.2—dc20   92-8725
                                                           CIP
                                                            AC

Printed in the United States of America

2   4   6   8   10   9   7   5   3   1

For the Cassano family—
Sherry, Graham, Chris, and Tim

CONTENTS

HUSKINGS, QUILTINGS, AND BARN RAISINGS

1

MANY HANDS MAKE LIGHT WORK

One early fall morning in upper New York State, a group of friends gathered to raise the roof on a newly built barn. When the roof was finally in place, they gave a cheer. Then they ate a hearty meal prepared by the owners of the barn. Many of the foods served—the potatoes, green beans, tomatoes, cucumbers, and fruit—came from the family's garden and orchard. This roof raising, followed by an afternoon of food and good times, took place in 1991. Those who participated were carrying on an American tradition that dates back to colonial days.

Diaries and other written accounts of life in colonial and pioneer days describe apple-paring parties, husking bees, wood-sawing contests, barn raisings, reaping contests, thread-spinning contests, knitting bees, soap boilings, fish and meat smokings, bean stringings, maple sugaring-off celebrations, and house raisings, among other work-play parties.

In the late 1700s, a French immigrant named Hector Crèvecoeur observed the cooperation that enabled people to build new lives in North America. From 1760 to 1769, Crèvecoeur had traveled widely in the Canadian and American colonies; then he began farming near what is now New York City. Crèvecoeur wrote to his family:

> Are we afraid, for example, that we shall not be able to break up our summer fallow [plowed land]? In due time, we invite a dozen neighbors, who will come with their teams and finish it all in one day. At dinner we give them . . . pies, puddings, fowls, roasted and boiled. . . . If any of our wives are unable to spin that quantity of flax which was intended, they give out one pound to every one of their acquaintances. The youngsters take the same quantity. . . . The day is fixed when they all bring home the yarn to the house and receive in return a hearty supper and a dance. The same is one for every species of labor. . . . Thus we help one another; thus by our single toils at home and by our collective strength we remove any obstacles which no single family could do.

People who came to North America had to meet their needs for shelter, food, and clothing in strange, new surroundings. Not only had these people left their homes behind; but the crowded passenger ships that carried them across the ocean had little space for personal belongings. They brought only necessities and a few items they could not bear to leave behind. Likewise, those who journeyed westward across the continent loaded the most important items into their covered wagons or onto pack animals. These pioneers knew that they would probably have to cross fast-moving waters and rough mountain ranges.

A typical covered wagon in the early 1800s held certain basic items. There were cooking utensils, such as an iron kettle and skillet, a butter churn, a corn grater, candlesticks, and a teapot. Just as important were a rifle with ammunition and some metal tools, including a knife, hoe, and ax. Each family member needed some warm clothes and bedding. In order to start growing their own food quickly, settlers packed seeds and farm tools. Room was made for the family Bible and a few other treasures: books, small musical instruments such as violins, perhaps a favorite toy for each child. A lucky family might squeeze in a log cradle and a rocking chair.

Of course, they needed enough food to survive the journey. They took bacon, coffee, dried beef, cornmeal, dried beans, dried fruit, sugar, and salt, and sacks filled with feed for their domestic animals. Small traps were used to catch game they could cook and eat along the way. The travelers also picked berries and nuts and fished in streams.

Often, the settlers' animals did not survive the journey. In a diary she kept during her family's 1854 trip to Oregon, Amelia Stewart Knight, a wife and mother of eight children, described the losses of cattle and oxen:

April 17: "Lost our muley cow."

May 17: "We had a dreadful storm of rain and hail last night and vey sharp lightning. It killed two oxen for one man. . . ."

August 1: "This evening another of our best milk cows died. . . . We are hardly ever out of sight of dead cattle on this side of the Snake River. . . ."

August 12: "Lost one of our oxen. He dropped dead in the yoke."

Loss of livestock, bad weather, illness, hunger, and other hardships plagued the early settlers of North America. But they had determination and courage to make new homes in what was often a wilderness.

North America was rich in natural resources and held many opportunities, but some colonists had already been warned about the large amount of work they would have to do. There was plenty of wood in the forests, but it had to be cut and carried, then burned as firewood or shaped into houses and barns. There was good soil, but it first had to be cultivated. One warning to would-be emigrants, published in England, said, "I would have no man trusting too much to the fertility of the bounds where he is to go, and too little to his own . . . industry."

Industry—hard work—enabled people to provide their own housing, food, clothing, and other necessities. New settlements held no ready-built houses; no markets with dairy products, meats, or produce; and no shops selling furniture, blankets, fabrics, or clothes. Besides, most settlers did not have money to buy these things. Few coins were in circulation, and most people paid for things by trading goods or services rather than using cash. Instead of buying things, families worked to grow, build, and make what they needed. They used whatever materials they could find or save, trying not to let anything go to waste.

Like people everywhere, the settlers enjoyed getting together with friends, so they could share jokes, news, stories, and ways of dealing with problems. There was little free time for fun or socializing alone, with so many chores always waiting to be done. It seemed natural to combine chores with a social event, and the various work-play parties were the result. People planned ways to do chores together.

Hard work seemed to go faster when people laughed, exchanged recipes and ideas, and looked forward to the food and fun that would follow. The tasty food ranged from cider and fried chicken to beef potpies, pancakes, and freshly pulled taffy. The fun included games, contests, sports, singing, and dancing.

Many work-play parties helped neighbors in

need. Some people needed help because they were newly arrived and had to establish a home and farm; others, because they were going through hard times, such as a fire or an illness in the family.

After visiting some frontier settlements in 1835, an Englishman named Charles Latrobe wrote, "A life in the woods teaches many lessons, and this among the rest, that you must both give assistance to your neighbor, and receive it in return, without either grudging or pouting."

Hard work and cooperation were keys to surviving in new and challenging places. The resourceful settlers found ways to get their work done and have some fun in the process. Besides showing the truth of the old saying "Many hands make light work," these early Americans came up with a proverb of their own: "A hard day's work makes a soft bed."

2

SETTLING IN

New neighbors! To people living in sparsely settled areas in early America, these two words carried excitement. The arrival of new settlers enabled people to hear news about their former homelands or about other parts of the country. It also meant that everyone living within several miles around the area would soon gather to help the new arrivals clear their land and build a home, and perhaps a barn.

Clearing the land was a strenuous job, especially without enough work animals or equipment. Yet the land had to be at least partially cleared to make way for a house, other farm buildings, and crops. There also had to be enough space among the trees where the sun could provide light for growing crops.

Several work-play parties were held to clear

land. One, called a chopping bee, was often held for a man who had just gotten married or for families who had just arrived. A call went out for all able-bodied men in the area to attend. Some of them walked or rode to the party from as far away as 10 miles to arrive early in the morning, bringing their sharpest axes.

Soon, the sounds of repeated chopping filled the air. With forceful swings of their axes, the men worked to clear enough land for the new residents. At the end of the day, a drive was sometimes held in order to knock over several large trees at the same time. Drives were both suspenseful and dangerous. The trunks of a group of trees were partially cut, then bound together with rope. The more daring men

began tugging on the rope to pull down the group of trees all at once. Accidents and even deaths occasionally resulted from a drive. But some men took the risk rather than wait to fell one tree at a time.

Some settlers used a method called windrow felling to clear land more quickly. Windrow felling means chopping trees so that they fall down in rows, then pushing the rows together to make one or more large piles. The resulting piles of trees were burned. Afterward, a farmer could pull out the smaller stumps that remained in the ground or use gunpowder, if he had it, to blast out stumps. Women and children helped to cut smaller trees and bushes with a small ax or a bushwhack, a metal tool with sharp edges that was often used to chop away underbrush. Dense underbrush was piled up and burned.

After a large enough opening was made in the land, usually during the spring, a family could start farming. Sandford C. Cox, a settler in an area near the upper Wabash River during the early 1800s, later wrote that he and his neighbors "cleared lands, rolled logs, and burned brush, blazed out paths from one cabin to another." In Wabash country, settlers like Cox found tall sycamore, oak, and tulip trees that took a great deal of effort to remove.

In Vermont, work-play parties to chop down trees were called mowing bees. In *Tales of Vermont Ways and People,* Bertha S. Dodge quotes from a nineteenth-century settler's diary: "It was no uncommon occurrence for from 5 to 8 acres of heavy timbered land to be logged off in a single bee. . . .

Twenty to 25 scythes [hand-held cutting tools with long curved blades] was a common field force; and all these in full clip, all in stroke, laying their well-mown swaths right round the meadow."

Sometimes fallen trees were left in place to dry out all summer. The farm owner worked busily into the autumn, when there might be a piling bee, a work-play party at which people removed and discarded stumps. The tops of the dead, fallen trees were set on fire and the lighter tree limbs burned out, leaving charred trunks still rooted in the ground. At the bee, the men and their oxen or horses pulled out the largest, most stubborn stumps. Oxen were hitched to chains tied around the stumps. As the oxen kept circling the stumps, the roots were twisted out of the ground.

Another method used at piling bees was to place small sticks of wood across the tops of very large logs to burn through them. This left shorter lengths that could be removed more easily. One useful side effect of burning the trees was that their ashes enriched the soil, making for better crops.

Just as necessary as a chopping bee in some places was the stone hauling or stone bee. Settlers dug and yanked rocks from the fields, where they were too numerous for a farmer to plant crops. One family and their oxen could not do this chore alone in New England and other places that had very rocky soil.

A work-play party called a house raising was held to meet the basic need for shelter. Upon arriving at the place they planned to settle, people sometimes made a temporary shelter called a lean-to—an open-faced shelter made by laying a cross timber across two trees or forked posts. Saplings were laid down from the cross timber to a large log to make a sloped roof. The sides were built up with logs, brush, and clay mud. Soil and brush added more warmth to the roof. This provided a place to live, however rough, until the family could clear enough land and gather the materials they needed for a cabin.

Settlers looked forward to building their own log cabins, which were more comfortable places to live. Before they could build a cabin, they needed enough logs (often ash, beech, maple, or poplar) that were nearly the same size. These logs had to be cut to the proper length, then pulled to the site of the future cabin. There they waited until the day the neighbors arrived for the cabin raising.

In *The Old Northwest: Pioneer Period, 1815–1840,* R. Carlyle Buley says, "Although many an isolated settler was forced by laborious methods to roll up the logs into place and erect his small cabin by his own efforts, as a rule the cabin raising was accomplished by the co-operative efforts of the neighbors."

People built different styles of homes, depending upon the times they lived and the materials available. For example, a seventeenth-century New Englander preparing for a house raising might first plan a home, commonly one room in size, with a cellar below that would provide food storage and help keep the house warm. Then he put aside enough timber to build the home and readied a stone foundation. Stone, plentiful in New England, was also used for chimneys. A wooden sill, made of squared timbers, was then made to fit over the foundation. When the remaining timbers, upper beams, and posts for the house were shaped, the settler got a supply of treenails—pegs carved out of tree wood. Then he asked his neighbors to the raising party.

At the "raisin'," the men usually did the work that required the most physical strength. They divided themselves into groups, according to their special talents. One group was assigned to raise the front wall of the house; another group raised the back wall. The men pushed the sides up, as far as their arms could reach, then used long poles called pikes to press them into place. Yet another small group stood down in the cellar and used pikes to keep the frames from bending too far inward. A team of workers held the walls in place while others pounded the nails into them. Women and children carried nails and tools to the workers. At last, the frame was done. Now, the owners had to finish the new home.

Wood frame houses like these, with side beams and heavy rafters to support the roof, were most common in New England and Pennsylvania. These homes usually were constructed with a ridgepole—a board that went across the top of the roof. After the ridgepole was in place, it was customary to put a green branch at each end. Sometimes the owners decided to name the new house. As part of this custom, one of the men sat on the roof astride the ridgepole and recited this rhyme:

> Here's a mighty fine frame
> Which deserves a good name
> Say what shall we call it?

After the house raising, the settlers helped themselves to roasted game, breads and other baked goods, and fruits and vegetables that were in season. The food was prepared by the women and served from tables that had been set up outdoors. The hosts knew that their helpers would be hungry after such strenuous work.

During the 1800s, in the western frontier areas, neighbors joined together to raise a log cabin. Some took up to three days to build. During that time, the families ate their meals together and enjoyed shooting contests, races, dances, and other activities. Such an event was a welcome break from the often lonely existence of the western settlers. The women and girls of the settlement might spend weeks preparing the food that would be served.

As was true at the colonial house raising, the men worked in teams, some cutting trees and shaping logs, some putting up the beams and frames. Those with special skills made tools, including hammers and saws, and shingles fashioned from shaved bark. When the framework was finished, a group raised it into place. The large beams were raised and positioned by ropes, with everyone pulling on them.

The four best builders were designated as the corner men. They had to notch the logs at the corners and see to it that the walls were erected squarely and evenly. Others helped by carrying logs and equipment to places they were needed. There was plenty of noise and laughter as people of all ages carried out their tasks against a background of steadily pounding hammers. The workers stopped from time to time for a drink of cider, usually brought to them by children who darted back and forth, refilling the mugs.

A finished log cabin was usually about 15 feet wide and 20 feet long. It stood anywhere from 7 to 14 feet high because lifting the heavy logs much higher than that was difficult. After the logs were in place, family members, including children, chinked— filled—the cracks to keep out the rain and cold weather. Mud, grass, moss, leaves, and straw were used for chinking cracks.

There was little furniture inside the cabins, at least in the beginning. For that reason, settlers often built their cabins around flat stumps that they could use as instant tables. Oiled paper from England was highly prized for covering open windows. The cabin also had a doorway, facing south to make the most of the sunlight. Animal skins or blankets were hung there until the owners could make a wooden door.

With the roof finally in place, the participants were ready on the last evening for music and fun. Often, the men drank toasts to the new house, to America, and to one another. A typical cabin-raising supper included roasted rabbit, squirrel, turkey, deer, and other game, along with seasonal vegetables, corn bread, cookies, gingerbread, pies, and baked puddings. One North Carolina house raising in the mid-1800s featured fried chicken, ham, sweet potatoes, buttered hominy grits, peas, tomatoes, green beans, biscuits with gravy, molasses, coffee, pies, and cakes.

The neighbors sang and danced to the accompaniment of a fiddle or two. "Yankee Doodle" and "The Liberty Song" were among the most popular musical choices. In some parts of the South, where religious beliefs forbade the use of musical instruments, people sang without them.

Late in the night, the activities ended and people started for home. Those who lived too far away left early the next morning. At home, the settlers resumed their own chores, looking forward to the next opportunity to socialize with their neighbors.

3

RAISING THE BARN

In 1795, a Vermont settler wrote about an unfortunate but not uncommon event in his neighborhood:

Mr. Stephen Hollister's barn was burned by sparks blowing from a neighbor's clearing. The neighbors who rallied at the burning determined that he should have a new barn. They scattered to invite others and to return with tools, team, provisions, &c., next morning. . . . The timber was cut, hewed, framed and raised in a day; and before the ruins were done smoking, a new barn frame, 30 feet by 40 feet, was ready for covering.

This diary entry, quoted by Bertha S. Dodge in *Tales of Vermont Ways and People,* shows how settlers united in times of trouble. Fires occurred frequently in early America and led to the damage and loss of both homes and barns. Usually, however, a barn raising signaled a happier occasion—for example, a marriage or the arrival of a new family in the area. Barn raisings were among the most festive work-play parties. People of all ages participated in the work, feasting, and fun.

Barn raisings were traditional among the German and Dutch immigrants who settled in various parts of North America. Many Germans were experienced farmers who knew the value of providing a barn to house animals during cold weather.

Farmers prepared for a barn raising by first digging and preparing a foundation, usually of stone. Sometimes, they also laid the walls and prepared the rafters—sloping beams that support the roof of a building—and other needed lumber. The goal of the barn raising was to erect the barn's heavy wood framework with the united strength of the group. It was up to the owner to complete the rest without help.

Like house raisings, barn raisings began early in the morning, and people were assigned to tasks that made the most of their skills. If the lumber had not been prepared earlier, some men began by cutting down trees; others made them into beams and boards. A team laid down boards to made the barn floor. Against a chorus of sawing and pounding, the

big beams of the barn's frame were fitted and nailed together on the ground. Long wooden poles called pikes were used to push the heavy pieces of the barn's frame into place.

In "Home Life in Early Indiana," William F. Vogel describes how a midwestern barn raising was organized: "The neighbors divided themselves into choppers, hewers, carpenters, and masons. Those who found it impossible to report for duty might pay an equivalent in nails, boards, or other materials." In other words, a neighbor unable to work that day felt obligated to contribute something to the new barn.

A completed barn was nearly always the largest building on the property. It might measure 66 feet long by 34 feet wide, with walls standing 16 feet high. With a sturdy barn in place, the family had a shelter for horses and cows they had or hoped to have in the future. Hay, corn, and other grains could be kept dry in the barn.

Lemonade and cider, along with cookies, were typically served during the barn raising. The workers sat down for a hearty lunch and for an evening meal if the work ended at night. The food served depended on the time of year and the region of the country. A German-American barn raising might include soup with dumplings, ground-meat sausages, wurst, pickled cabbage and eggs, potatoes, *schnitz und knep* (dried apples and dumplings), applesauce, cider, bread, apple butter, and fruit preserves.

The women in the group had the task of preparing and serving the dinner. It gave them a chance

to share their best homemade breads, cakes, pies, and cookies. If fresh or dried fruits were scarce, they might make pie fillings out of something else—squash sweetened with honey or molasses, or mincemeat prepared with bear or venison (deer meat) instead of the usual beef. Children helped to prepare and serve the food, in addition to carrying supplies and beverages to the men building the barn.

After the meal, the workers rested until they felt energetic enough to take part in games. One favorite contest was a wrestling match. The smallest boys began this contest, with the losers dropping out and the new winners wrestling each other. By and by, the older boys joined in, followed by the men. Whoever was left at the end was declared the

winner. Games of horseshoes, target shooting, and footraces were also popular. There were contests to see who would jump the highest and the longest distances.

Young people looked forward to the dance that often took place late in the evening. Barn dances were one of the main occasions for courting among men and women old enough to marry. These events gave them a chance to meet and spend time together. Sometimes, a young man escorted his favorite young lady to her home.

The barn dance was originally called a *bran* dance, because grain—in this case, corn kernels—was thrown on the rough new floor. As the dancers' feet moved across the barn's floor, they pressed oil out of the corn kernels, helping to smooth and polish the raw boards. So even the dancing at a barn raising served a useful purpose.

Musicians on the fiddle, banjo, zither, guitar, or accordion played tunes such as "Sugar in the Gourd," "Fisher's Hornpipe," "Barbara Allen," "Sour Wood Mountain," "Turkey in the Straw," and "Old Dan Tucker." A fiddler-caller positioned the couples for square dances, waved his bow merrily, and told the dancers to "look lively now" as one tune followed another.

A break in the dancing featured more refreshments—cider, cold meats, apples, and pastries. The barn had been raised, and, with the custom of the "bran" dance, the new building had been warmed by the neighbors as well.

4

HARVEST TIME

For Americans of colonial and frontier days, getting enough to eat was often an ongoing problem. Most of their daily activities centered on getting and fixing food—hunting or fishing, planting, harvesting, preserving, storing, and cooking. People in every region knew of a "starving time," most often in the winter, when there had not been enough to eat. The lack of food led to illnesses and deaths in various settlements.

Often, new colonists arrived in America hungry. The food on their ships ran out or was of such poor quality that the immigrants became weak, sick, and exhausted. This caused more problems, because weak, sick people had trouble finding and raising the food they needed. The same thing happened to many westbound settlers, whose food supply ran out when the weather, terrain, or other conditions along the way slowed them down.

Not surprisingly, most work-play parties involved preparing and preserving food. Animals had to be butchered, the meat smoked or pickled; fruits were peeled, sliced, and dried. Even slices of autumn pumpkins could be used months later, if they were first dried. Several important parties involved staple foods—apples, corn, molasses, beans, and maple sugar. In a related task, children went "a-leafing" in the autumn to gather oak leaves that would be used all winter as mats for cakes and bread loaves baking inside the fireplace's brick oven.

Early Americans had to be resourceful and open-minded as they learned to use and enjoy foods in their new environment. In the 1700s, a visitor to New York State described tasting a dish that was new to him but that his hosts had learned to use when more conventional game was scarce. Of his raccoon meal, the visitor said, "It was very fat and of a good flavor, almost like a pig."

Chief among the crops that people learned to raise in America was corn, a food that saved many from starving. Native Americans had cultivated this nutritious and hardy plant for centuries. In 1608, at the Jamestown colony in Virginia, Captain John Smith planted 40 acres of corn with the help of Powhatan Indians. Pilgrim leader William Bradford wrote in his book *Of Plimoth Plantation* of the "grim and grizzled faces of starvation" during the winter of 1620–21.

Aided by a Pawtuxet Indian named Squanto, who demonstrated "how to set it, and after, how to dress and tend it," the Plymouth colonists planted corn in the spring of 1621. It kept them alive during their first two years. Near the end of a harsh winter, they rationed corn to five *kernels* per person a day.

The Indians also showed new arrivals how to grind and cook corn. They pounded the kernels in a hollowed stone to make a coarse meal, which they sifted in a basket. Large chunks were pounded and resifted. Many corn recipes kept their Indian names through the years: pone, succotash, hominy, supawn, and samp, for example.

After settlers began raising substantial crops, they started working together to husk corn and prepare it for the grinder or mill. In Massachusetts, in 1767, a farmer named Ames wrote in his diary that "there is a Custom amongst us of making an Entertainment at husking of Indian Corn . . . and after the Corn is finished they . . . give three cheers or huzza . . . [and] after a hearty Meal about 10 at Night they go to their pastimes."

Cornhusking parties involved both men and women. At harvest time, neighbors usually met at dusk in the barn and sat around a long pile of corn. They formed two teams, sometimes choosing members by flipping a chip that had been made by leaving bark on one side and filing the other side smooth. The team leaders then agreed on how to divide the corn pile into equal parts, placing a marker in the middle.

As the contest began, fingers moved quickly

and dozens of ears hit the door. Some workers used husking pins—small spikes fastened across their palms—to help them remove the outer leaves of the corn. The huskers talked, joked, and sang folk songs as they hurried to finish their pile first.

Occasionally, a young man found a red ear in his corn. This permitted him to kiss a girl at the bee. When a girl found a red ear, she could hand it to her favorite young man and receive a kiss from him. Married people kissed each other. Some unattached young men took care to hide a red ear in their pockets before going "a husking."

As the work continued, each side watched the dwindling piles of corn. A shout of triumph and cheers for the winning team's leader rang out as the last ear was husked.

Luke Woodard of Indiana described the cornhusking party in a poem for his book *Pioneer Days*:

'Twas fun and useful industry combined. . . .
The hour passed on, and forward went the work,
Off went the husks, with grip, rip, and a jerk,
The ears were tossed into the crib, and lower,
Each moment grew the unhusked pile before,
While larger grew the husk pile in the rear,
When lo! at nine the barn floor was all clear!

After the husking, a late dinner was served on pine boards laid across trestles. Meat and vegetable potpies, roast lamb and pig, beans, peas, applesauce, pies, puddings, and preserves were among the dishes served at the huskings, along with tea and cider. Sometimes there was popcorn, prepared over an open fire and seasoned with salt and butter or bacon grease. After supper came games and contests—running and jumping races and "throwing the hammer"—seeing who could throw a hammer the farthest. A square dance ended the cornhusking party.

The settlers also got together to pare and cut apples that would be used and stored for winter. These parties were called apple parings, apple cuts, or apple bees. Apples were treasured for their delicious taste and because they could be used in different ways. Many settlers took apple seeds and saplings to plant in areas with no fruit trees. With luck, there would be plenty of apples to harvest and pare every fall.

Part of the apple harvest was eaten raw. Remaining fruits were baked or cooked—into apple butter, sauce, pies, cakes, cookies, stuffings, dumplings, crisps, and strudels. Apple dishes had colorful names, like pandowdy (a two-crusted pie), cobbler (sliced sweetened apples with a biscuit topping), and slump (cooked sweetened apples with dumplings). Cider and vinegar were made from bruised apples and cores, with the pigs getting whatever was left.

Dr. Aurelius, who visited a Swedish settlement in Delaware in 1758, wrote: "Apple-pie is used through the whole year, and when fresh apples are no longer to be had, dried ones are used. It is the evening meal of children." Dr. Aurelius also wrote about "house-pie," an apple pie with a crust so strong it "is not broken if a wagon wheel goes over it."

Colonial apple bees were described by Hector Crèvecoeur:

> In the fall of the year, we dry great quantities, and this is one of those rural occupations which most amply reward us. Our method is this: we gather the best kind. The neighboring women are invited to spend the evening at our house. A basket of apples is given to each of them, which they peel, quarter, and core. These peelings and cores are put into another basket and when the

intended quantity is thus done, tea, a good
supper, and the best things we have are served
up. . . . The quantity I have thus peeled is
commonly twenty bushels which gives me about
three of dried ones.

Sometimes, both men and women took part in
frontier apple bees. Often, only women attended,
forming a circle around a washtub, with aprons tied
over their homespun or calico dresses. They shared
stories, recipes, songs, and common problems as
they pared and sliced, tossing the peels and fruit into
separate pans and baskets placed around the kitchen.

Young girls tried to pare a whole apple in a
single peel. By custom, they flung the peel over their

left shoulder. A peel that landed unbroken was thought to form the first initial of the parer's future mate, or, as the saying went, "Peel it in one curl and see the initial of your true love."

After the apples were pared and cut, the slices were dried by various methods. Some people strung them on linen thread and hung them on rafters in the kitchen, attic, or in front of the house. Other people laid the fruit slices in single layers on a wood rack outdoors and kept turning them over in the sun until they dried. When winter came, the dried slices could be soaked in water overnight, which made them swell to their former size. Then they were cooked as usual.

Cut fruit that was not dried could be made into sauce or apple butter and stored. Favored combinations of sweet and sour apples were placed in a kettle, along with molasses or another sweetener to taste. The sauce was cooked and stirred over an open fire in the fireplace. Sauce, stored in barrels in the cellar, often froze during the winter, resulting in an icy food the settlers also enjoyed eating. Apple butter was made by cooking pared fruit with cider. Some homemakers spent days cooking their apples.

Apples and other fruits were a welcome addition to meals in early America. In those days, appeasing a "sweet tooth" was not always easy. White sugar had to be imported from the West Indies. A loaf came in the form of a large white cone weighing 8 to 10 pounds, and with care a family might make it last a year. In the 1700s, a sugar loaf cost more than a dollar, an amount that could buy a family a year's worth of flour. Those who could afford to buy white sugar often saved it for holiday treats or for special occasions, such as when visitors came to tea.

Luckily, the settlers learned about an important natural sweetener from Native Americans. New England colonists saw that the Algonquin tribes had a festive holiday when they gathered the sap of maple trees in large bark containers. They cooked the sap in wooden troughs by dropping in hot stones, which caused the liquid to steam and gradually turn into a thicker, sweet syrup.

In 1706, Governor Berkeley of Virginia wrote:

The Sugar-Tree yields a kind of sap or juice which by boiling is made into sugar. The Juice is drawn out, by wounding the Trunk of the Tree, and placing a Receiver under the Wound. It is said that the Indians make one Pound of sugar out of eight Pounds of the Liquor.

Maple sap—or "sweet water"—is found in sugar maple trees and is produced by the changing temperatures. Cold nights combined with warm days make the sap start to run, so the sap season is in late winter when winters are mild and in early spring when winters are harsh.

To get ready for sugaring, New Englanders began checking their maple trees in mid-February, looking for a clear liquid on the ends of the twigs. Maple sap is about 1 to 6 percent sugar, the rest being mostly water. Tree owners hoped for a "good run" each year.

Young boys often helped to drive spouts into the trees and place troughs beneath them. A notch was made in the tree trunk about 4 to 5 feet above the ground. It held a spout that would guide the running sap into the container below. Early colonists used troughs made of butternut logs, hollowed out as the Native Americans did it, under the spouts. These troughs were reused every year. Later on, people used buckets to hold the sap, which amounted to about two pailfuls a day in a full-grown maple. That amount of sap, boiled down, yielded about a pound of maple syrup.

For days after the sap began to run, men and boys emptied the containers regularly and carried tubs of sap to an outdoor clearing where syrup would be boiled over an open fire. The kettles hung on heavy sticks of green wood placed across strong, low trees. People at the sugaring site kept busy carrying troughs or buckets back and forth and bringing more dry wood for the fires underneath the sap kettles.

On the last afternoon or evening of the cooking process, families came from neighboring farmhouses for the sugaring-off party. Tinkling bells announced the horse-drawn sleighs full of neighbors. In *Golden Tales of New England,* May Lamberton Becker includes an account of a sugaring-off in Massachusetts, written by a young woman called Jemima:

A pleasant sleigh ride of four or five miles brought us to the domicile of friend H. . . . Arrived at the camp, we found two huge iron kettles suspended on a pole, which was supported by crotched stakes driven in the ground, and each half full of boiling syrup. . . . A steady fire of oak bark was burning underneath the kettles, and the boys and girls, friend H's sons and daughters, were busily engaged in stirring the syrup and replenishing the fire.

At the sugaring-off, Jemima and her friends used large brass tools called scummers to remove the scum that rose to the top of the boiling sap. Women and children usually took turns standing beside the boiling kettles to skim off any dirt or twigs that fell in. If the sap boiled so rapidly that it threatened to bubble over, they added a bit of lard to slow it down. In time, much of the water in the thin, pale liquid bubbled away, leaving a sweet, golden syrup.

The syrup was tested by dropping spoonfuls of it onto the snow. Experienced sugar makers could pick up the pieces, roll them between thumb and forefinger, and decide if the syrup was done. When it had boiled long enough, some syrup was poured into molds to harden, so that it could be saved and used as a sweetener. People dipped wooden paddles into a kettle to taste the syrup. But the highlight of the party, especially for young people, was the making of snow candy. Streams of the syrup were dribbled onto the snow. The sweet, waxy textured candy that resulted could be eaten at once or pulled like taffy.

To balance the sharp sweetness of the maple candy, a sour food—pickles—was served at the sugaring-off supper. Of course, there were plenty of doughnuts and pancakes that could be drenched with syrup. Other popular dishes included cottage cheese, deviled eggs, baked beans, milk, and hot coffee. Jemima and her friends enjoyed a dinner served on boards covered with snow white napkins and including "cold ham, tongue, pickles, bread, apple-sauce, preserves, doughnuts, butter, cheese, and potatoes," with hot chocolate to drink.

Memories of sugaring-off parties in Indiana prompted Luke Woodard to write in *Pioneer Days:*

And sugar-making time to me,
Was like an annual jubilee.
In iron kettles rudely swung;
On dogwood poles and forks, and hung,
'Twixt burning logs, day after day,
We boiled the liquid sweet away.
I watched the golden syrup boil,
And ever and anon the while,
With wooden paddle filled my cup
And dipped the waxy nectar up.

Another native sweetener that the settlers learned to make and use was molasses. In West Virginia, for example, the molasses boiling was held in September. Farmers usually planted a patch of sugarcane in the late spring when they planted their corn. In late September, they stripped the leaves from the green stalks before cutting them. Most farmers did not own the equipment needed to make molasses. They relied on someone who traveled to different groups of farms with a mill that contained large rollers to press the juice from the cane stalks and an evaporating pan in which the juice was boiled down to a thick texture.

People with small crops brought their cane to a centrally located farm. A single horse hitched to a pole walked around the mill in a circle. Raw juice flowed from the mill and was poured into the evaporating pan, heated by a wood fire below. People of all ages came at night for the "bilin" (boiling) party held to celebrate the event.

Rural West Virginia was also among the places where people attended bean stringings to help those with a large crop get their vegetables ready for canning and pickling. At bean stringings, people sat much as they did at apple bees—around a large washtub in which they could put their strung vegetables. Women prepared food for the bean stringings, frequently cooking taffy for a "pull." Young people grabbed handfuls of the sticky, soft chunks of taffy and pulled them until they became hard enough for candy. Baked goods were also served to the helper-guests.

West Virginia and some other regions had a soil and climate that enabled farmers to raise enough wheat for their family's use. The harvested wheat was ground at a local gristmill, a place where people could pay or barter to have machines grind their grain into flour. The resulting flour was made into biscuits, light bread, and pancakes.

Before threshing machines were available, people had to thresh their grain by flailing. The wheat was put in a large, square box with low sides and beaten with a flail—a short stick attached by a leather strip to a long wooden handle. Flailing became the focus of another food-related work party. Children old enough to use a flail properly were expected to help too.

After the threshing machine was invented, in 1834, men who owned such machines also traveled from farm to farm, threshing local farmers' wheat. About ten or twelve men were needed to harvest and thresh the wheat crops. They worked all day and into the night, then ate a big meal called a supper, prepared by the women and girls. Boys kept busy too, doing the other farm chores and gathering firewood for the cooking stoves. At threshing parties, the men usually went to sleep after supper. They were too tired for contests or games.

Food was featured at other work-play parties. In areas where people raised pigs, a butchering-off might be held to smoke and salt the meat for winter, make sausages, and pickle other parts of the animal, such as the feet. Such preserved meats could be kept safely through the winter months in those days before refrigeration was available. Hog and pig fat—lard—was kept to be used for cooking.

Neighbors left the butchering-off with some meat for their own use. Preserved meats and other foods were important, because without preserving the foods would spoil. The first canned foods were not made until 1812, in England. Canned foods were not widely produced in the United States until the late 1860s, and refrigerators were not available until the 1900s.

These types of work-play parties enabled early Americans to prepare and save their own foods, which was more economical than buying them. The parties were also like small harvest festivals—times and places to celebrate together, knowing there would be food on the table in the coming months.

5

KEEPING WARM

One of the best-known work-play parties, the quilting bee, has been the object of songs, stories, and poems. The famous nineteenth-century American composer Stephen Foster featured this work-play party in one of his folk songs:

> In the sky the bright stars glittered,
> On the banks the pale moon shone,
> And 'twas from Aunt Dinah's quilting party,
> I was seeing Nellie home.

Quilts are made of two pieces of fabric, with padding material in between, held together with stitching. Nobody is sure when the first quilt was made, but the craft dates back at least to 5000 B.C.

Spinning and weaving produced the first cloth along the Ganges, Euphrates, and Nile rivers, and people learned to sew cloth pieces together. The need for warmth led people to layer fabrics and attach them.

In the eleventh and twelfth centuries, crusaders saw these layered covers in the Middle East and took them to Europe. People in Europe learned to make and use quilted clothing and bedclothes. They also "patched" scraps together, an idea that arose when woven cloth wore out in places, leaving the remainder still too good to throw away. Quilts became more decorative, with vivid colors and central ornaments and patterns with scrolls, flowers, leaves, vines, and geometric designs.

First English, then Dutch, German, and Scandinavian immigrants brought their crafts to North America. Quilting changed in the new homeland to suit the different materials, regions, and conditions. Colonial and frontier women were expert needleworkers who often could spin thread and weave and dye their cloth as well as sew it. An early American saying warned people not "to sit in idleness," so women of all social classes, in the city or country, did quilting and other kinds of needlework.

In frontier areas, cloth goods were expensive and hard to get. It took several years to grow enough flax (a fiber used to make linen cloth) or to raise enough sheep for their wool. When clothing or bedclothes wore out, thrifty homemakers patched them with other cloth pieces. Patching was also necessary when people did not have enough fabric for a whole quilt background piece upon which they could sew decorations. Patchwork quilts, with covers or tops made entirely of pieces, thus were developed. Quilting was done daily in most American homes during the 1800s and was an obvious activity for a work-play party.

Quilting bees let women socialize and use their artistic and sewing skills, while providing household essentials. Often, quilts were the brightest and most individual items in pioneer homes. They used fabric that might otherwise have been discarded. Old clothes sewn in gave the quilts sentimental value too—as when scraps of Grandmother's wedding dress, a military coat, or a baby's christening gown were passed on in family quilts. Even scraps less than one inch square were used, with one quilt from the early 1800s containing 30,000 such tiny pieces.

Quilting bees were mostly winter events and were one of the few approved social outings for women. The quiltings often took place at the largest home nearby. Women brought their completed quilt tops and linings the same size, ready to be tied to a frame and sewn to the bottom layer.

Young girls could attend quilting bees. By four years of age, many had learned to sew, and some made their first quilts at age five. Often, a quilting bee was the only social activity during the long winter months. In *Quilt of Many Stars,* a story about an 1841 bee in Ohio, twelve-year-old Rebecca Lefferts is delighted when a neighbor comes to her family's snow-bound cabin in the woods to announce: "There is to be a quilting at our house today, and I thought you would like to come. . . . I have broken a path so you can come right along back with me."

Arriving at the bee, Rebecca found a fire blazing in the kitchen fireplace and other girls sewing patterned quilt tops. They "sat about on stools with their bags of bright scraps of cloth—orange, yellow, snuff-color, maroon, plum, purple, and lavender—carefully stitching the patches that would sometime be joined together to make their own quilts."

A woman who attended the same bee, at the home of Mary Scott, later wrote to friends back in Connecticut: "Everybody turned out. She had two big turkeys and her famous currant jelly. One of Mary's new quilts is called the Star-and-Crescent. She got it from Mrs. Lefferts, one of the new Pennsylvania Dutch families."

Any young woman about to marry was expected to have finished twelve quilts and an extra quilt top. This last top often had a border and a special design made up of bells, hearts, and flowers. A bride-to-be brought this quilt top to her engagement party, and neighbors finished the wedding quilt for the young couple.

Quiltings started early in the morning. As many as twelve women set to work at the quilting frame. The frame consisted of four wooden bars, each about 10 feet long, formed into a square with pieces of wood extending from all four corners. These wood pieces were placed in the slats of four chairs so that the quilt could be kept flat and set at a convenient height.

After the quilt top was padded with layers of wool or cotton and placed squarely over the lining, the fabrics were basted—sewn loosely—together. The quilt was attached to the four sides of the frame with coarse thread or twine. The sewing began, with the best needlewomen making small, even stitches on as many as seven or eight quilts. Thousands of stitches might go into each quilt, and sometimes the stitching itself was planned to create a design. They followed the design chosen by the quilt's owner.

Early patched quilts were fitted together in a

random way to make crazy or hit-and-miss designs. Later, more intricate, organized designs developed, many of them using geometric patterns. Dutch settlers of New Amsterdam, the territory that was later called New York City, made neatly stitched designs on backgrounds of imported cloth. Germans in Pennsylvania made their own hand-loomed cloth with bold designs. Frontier women who lacked cotton wadding might stuff their quilts with grasses, cornhusks, straw, or milkweed.

While they worked, the women exchanged patterns, planned designs, and traded pieces of calico cloth in order to get the colors and patterns they wanted to use in their quilts. News of one another's families, recent sermons of the circuit minister, wedding plans, and upcoming political elections might be discussed. Girls too young to sew the quilts sat on the floor nearby making strips of rags into rugs.

Foot by foot, each side of the quilt was finished and rolled up on its bar so that another section could be sewn. Ordinary household items were used to mark designs—a plate for a round object like a wreath, for instance. Patterns for quilt designs were cut from hard cardboard or tin. The Log Cabin, Roman Square, Philadelphia Pavement, Shoofly, Double Wedding Ring, and Star of Bethlehem were popular patterns. Some quilts are named for dance steps: Hands All Around and Swing to the Center are two examples.

A light luncheon of cakes, pickles, and preserves provided a short break at eleven o'clock. The women returned quickly to work, hoping to finish the quilts by five or six o'clock, when the men would arrive for supper and the party. A Pennsylvania quilting supper in the 1840s featured roasted wild turkey, currant relish, rye pancakes with honey, apple pies, and coffee. In her novel *The Minister's Wooing,* New England author Harriet Beecher Stowe wrote of an 1859 quilting supper that featured cold fowl, tongue, loaf cakes, doughnuts, berries, and cherries.

After supper, the men and women danced to fiddlers' tunes, while the boys and girls enjoyed

games. Sometimes the whole group played games with the finished quilts. One game involved putting the quilt around people's heads and having them try to find other people in the room. In another game, some of the lighter guests, including children, were wrapped in a quilt, then tossed in the air, to test the quilt's strength.

Quiltings were not always one-day events. Author Alice Morse Earle found that in Narragansett, in 1752, one quilting bee lasted ten days. If the weather was especially severe, guests at a one-day bee might

stay overnight, continuing their work the next day.

Women sometimes had a chance to display their finest quilts. There were quilting contests and exhibits at town and county fairs, to which the men took their best crops and livestock. Besides showing their handiwork to others, the women and girls might even hope to win a prize for a quilt with outstanding stitching and designs.

Besides making quilts together, the settlers met to perform other tasks that would provide clothing and bedding. Some frontier people wore clothing made from animal skins—deer, raccoon, squirrel, rabbit, bear, or buffalo—but wool was the main fabric used for clothing. Clothes were made of wool or linen (from the flax plant) or a combination of these called linsey-woolsey.

Cloth making began in the spring, when the sheep, wearing thick winter coats, were led to the riverbank to be washed. A mixture of tobacco and water was sometimes used, because it killed the bugs living in the sheep's fleece. Children who helped with this chore could enjoy going for a swim after they finished.

The freshly washed sheep were sheared, sometimes at a work-play party called a shearing. The most expert shearers could remove the fleece in one piece without cutting the animal. Then the sheared wool had to be cleaned, because sheep often accumulated burrs and tar in their coats that simple washing did not remove. Clean wool was moistened with lard oil so that it could be carded, or untangled. Two

rectangular paddles with wire teeth were used to card wool, one small bunch at a time, until it was evenly mixed. As with shearing, people with a lot of wool to card might form a work-play party for carding.

The carded fibers were spun, or twisted, into yarn on hand spindles or spinning wheels. The yarn was wound into coils or skeins that could be immersed in hot colorful dyes made from barks, nuts, flowers, or roots. The next step was to weave the cloth on a loom. The newly made cloth was then ready to be fulled, often at a fulling party. Woolen clothing would shrink later on unless it was first washed and fulled, a process that also made the fabric thicker and warmer.

To get ready for the fulling, a family soaked its cloth in a soap solution, then spread it on a table. People sat around the table, pulling, pushing, and twisting the fabric, while moving it in a circle. After two or three hours, the cloth was tighter and thicker. Another fulling method involved putting the soaked wool on the floor, where boys and girls danced up and down on it until it became soft and thick. Still other fulling parties had two rows of young men who stomped on the cloth with their bare feet until it was fulled. Songs, stories, jokes, and food added fun to this bee. The finished cloth was ready to be sewn into dresses, pants, and coats.

A party that produced material for bedding was the feather-stripping party. After geese were killed and plucked for food, early American housewives sorted the feathers carefully, according to size. Small feathers were used to stuff feather beds, while large quills were bagged and saved for a feather-stripping party that winter. Settlers stripped the soft down from piles of goose feathers. The down from these large feathers was used to stuff pillows, cushions, and quilts.

Whole families arrived on the cold, often snowy evening that had been chosen for the stripping. In the warm kitchen, adults sat working at a long table while the youngest children napped and the older children went outdoors to ice-skate.

Each pair of men and women sat beside an open pillowcase that had been pinned to the worktable. The woman steadied a basket on her knees to hold the discarded quills. Then everyone began to strip the down from the feathers as fast as he or she could by holding a feather by the tip with one hand and using the thumb and forefinger of the other hand to peel off the down. Each team raced to fill its pillowcase while people told stories, sang songs, and talked to help pass the time more quickly during this hard and untidy job.

The end of this frolic was often marked with popcorn and a taffy pull for the young people. Supper included roast goose, venison, biscuits, gingerbread, cider, and hot coffee. After a dance, the families returned home by sleigh or on foot.

Quilting bees, fulling parties, and feather-stripping parties were held in various parts of America. The warmer climate of the South favored the growth of the cotton plant, which yielded a fibrous material used for making cloth. After the cotton was picked, the fiber had to be separated from the seed. Although machines called gins were made for this purpose in the 1790s, some people had no gins and removed the seeds by hand, often in a group. *Folklore of American Holidays* quotes a description of a cotton-picking party from a diary written by Paul E. Doran:

> I went tonight to a cotton picking at Joe Sparks, the first one I ever attended. Many people here raise a small cotton patch for their own use. . . . they pick it by hand. . . . Cakes are baked, homemade candy is prepared, and the cotton is thoroughly dried in sacks by the fire. The old folks in one room, the youngsters in another, the picking begins. A prize is offered to the one who picks the most, a big slice of cake and some candy. All work feverishly until about 10 o'clock; then each person's cotton is weighed and the prize is awarded. Then candy and cake are passed, a song is sung, and all go home. . . . The old folks tell tales of their young days and the young laugh and enjoy themselves.

Other work-play parties of this type included sewing bees, spinning parties (at which fibers were spun into thread), and rag cuttings (to cut strips of old cloth used for rag rugs)—just about any activity that people would rather do together in order to make work more enjoyable.

6

WORK-PLAY PARTIES TODAY

On a summer morning, groups of people can be seen heading on foot or in horse-drawn carriages toward a neighbor's farm in Lancaster County, Pennsylvania, about 40 miles west of Philadelphia. The men are bearded and wear plain white or blue shirts, black trousers with suspenders, and flat-brimmed straw hats. The women are also simply dressed, in bonnets, longish dresses, and dark stockings. The men carry tools in their hands and pockets; the women and children carry baskets of food.

They have come to raise a new barn for a family whose old barn burned after being struck by lightning. An expert builder called a planner has laid out the building, taking into account the direction of the wind and the slope of the land. Some planners have built more than a hundred barns in their lifetimes and no longer even need to use a blueprint. After the foundation is in place, the men begin hammering and sawing as they build the walls, while the women and children do other chores.

Although this sounds like a scene from past centuries, it is a contemporary barn raising in an Amish farming community. The Amish and some other religious communities, such as the Mennonites (the Amish are an offshoot of the Mennonites), continue many customs of their ancestors, including a number of kinds of work-play parties.

Besides Pennsylvania, a number of Amish people live in Ohio, Indiana, Iowa, and Wisconsin. They

live simply, without plumbing or elecricity, with a horse and buggy providing most transportation. The Amish help one another in times of need, never relying on government assistance, which is against their religious beliefs. Community aid is at the heart of Amish life, and a barn raising is just one of the tasks for which neighbors unite. Together, they erect fences and farm structures, such as milk houses and smokehouses. They hold quilting bees, sewing bees, butchering parties, huskings, weeding parties, and other events at which they prepare fruits and vegetables for canning and drying.

On the day before a big work-play party such as a barn raising, some of the women come to the site to cook and bake. Others bring cakes, cookies, and pies with them the next morning. The smells of frying chicken and other foods fill the air as the men put the barn framework together using wooden pegs instead of metal nails.

As in barn raisings of the past, the men divide into groups, according to their talents, and put up the barn's framework and main timbers. There is a midmorning break to eat sandwiches, lemonade, doughnuts, and cookies. Later comes lunch, a larger meal, served on long tables—usually wooden planks laid on sawhorses—outdoors. This hearty meal may include a variety of meats, dairy products, and produce grown and preserved on the neighborhood farms: ham, chicken and gravy, mashed potatoes, celery, tomatoes, corn, pickles, baked beans, coleslaw, bread, cheese, grape preserves, apple butter, and coffee.

61

There are also abundant desserts, including fresh peaches, walnut pie, layer cake, and shoofly pie, an Amish specialty made with molasses.

As the sun sets, the barn frame is erect, and the farmer can finish it in the days that follow. Amish barns typically have two levels, with room for livestock, tools, hay, and corn, which is stored in the silo. The barn is built to last, and many have been passed on through several generations of the same family.

Outside Amish communities, barn raisings are held far less often than they were in earlier years, but the craft of quilting has remained popular throughout America. Sewing machines can now make the stitches that women did by hand in earlier days, but people continue to enjoy creating their own hand-sewn quilts. Women in all fifty states have formed quilting clubs and societies and sometimes join together to quilt at traditional bees. Local and nationwide quilting contests are also held, and an annual national quilting convention takes place in Paducah, Kentucky.

Quilts have sometimes been in the news during the twentieth century. Shortly after Herbert Hoover's election in 1928, Mercy Hospital in Kansas City benefited from quilting bees around the country. The hospital director, Dr. Katherine Richardson, had expressed a wish to use Double Irish Chain quilts on the charity children's hospital beds in the new wing, called Nurse Hall. Needlewomen around the country formed Mercy Hospital Clubs and hand-pieced 150 of the quilts in shades of blue and white.

In the 1930s, forty-nine Oklahoma women over age seventy-five, who had come to the state in the days when it was Indian Territory, made squares for a special historical quilt. When the top was finished, it was quilted at a bee at the Oklahoma governor's mansion. Mary Alice Murray, the governor's wife, presented the quilt to the state's historical society.

A small town in Connecticut chose to commemorate its 350th anniversary by displaying quilts at the historical society and explaining how they were made and used in earlier days. Part of the exhibit included photographs of quilting bees. Visitors were invited to sit down around a quilt set in a wood frame and add their own stitches to this "celebratory quilt."

Needlework has been used to make statements about social concerns. A long banner called the Peace Ribbon was sewn together to demonstrate the desire that many people in different countries have for world peace. Individuals and groups made thousands of banners, many of which were quilted, that described the things they cherished about life. The pieces were joined together to make a banner more than 10 miles long. Thousands of people gathered to watch the banner encircle the Pentagon building near Washington, D.C., at a peace demonstration in August 1985.

Another group of Americans planned and continue to make a quilt in memory of the thousands of people who have died as a result of AIDS (acquired immune deficiency syndrome). Besides being a memorial, the AIDS quilt is intended to raise public awareness about the suffering that AIDS has caused, leading to more funds for medical research.

Although people can sew or make quilts alone, using machines, the popularity of today's quilting groups shows a human desire to do useful creative work in the company of friends and neighbors. The popularity of hand-sewn quilts also shows that people appreciate one-of-a-kind objects that reflect the American heritage.

Whether in a rural area or an urban neighborhood, today's work-play parties can be an efficient and money-saving way to do a special task. The nonprofit organization Habitat for Humanity builds houses for people who cannot afford them. Former president Jimmy Carter, a skilled carpenter, and his wife, Rosalynn, are among the volunteers who have worked on this organization's group building projects. There are also work-play parties to build children's playgrounds and paint homes or community buildings. In several New York City neighborhoods, people plant and harvest community gardens together, as do other Americans who live in small towns and rural areas. People who are moving into a new house or apartment may find their friends helping with the move, then contributing food for a housewarming party.

Maple-sugaring parties are still held in New England, and some southern farmers hold molasses boilings like those they recall from childhood, even forgoing the use of modern equipment. One North Carolina farmer boils his syrup "the old way," using a horse to turn the machine that presses the sap from the sugarcane. He says he wants his children to share his happy childhood memories of "coming home from school to eat hot biscuits dripping with fresh molasses." And at one Vermont farm that welcomes visitors at sugaring-off time, people can enjoy the traditional candy on snow and eat pickles along with doughnuts dipped in fresh maple syrup.

In early America, people building new lives in new settlements relied on work-play parties to meet their basic needs. Today, people can meet those same needs by visiting numerous well-stocked stores. Yet quilting bees, sewing circles, harvest festivals, and the like are still popular. Although people today do not always need these events to survive, they like to socialize with neighbors and take part in community life. People also value the chance to share creative ideas and useful social skills and to see the results of their work, as in a quilt, community garden, or playground. So, despite the hectic pace of modern life—or perhaps because of it—people continue to plan ways to work and play together.

7

RECIPES

Here are some recipes to try at home. Some of these dishes are similar to those served at work-play parties. Others use foods, such as apples, that were featured at the food preparation parties. Be sure to ask a grown-up for help in preparing these dishes.

· SPOON BREAD ·

¼ cup yellow cornmeal
½ teaspoon salt
    (optional)
3 tablespoons melted
    butter

1 cup boiling water
1 cup milk
2 eggs, well beaten
1 teaspoon baking
    powder

Preheat oven to 350 degrees. Combine the ingredients in the order listed. Pour the batter into a 10-inch greased casserole and bake for about 40 minutes or until the bread is firm and has pulled from the edges of the pan. Makes 4 to 6 servings.

· JOHNNYCAKE ·

1 cup cornmeal
½ teaspoon salt
1 level teaspoon sugar
1 tablespoon butter

1½ cups boiling water
cream or milk
1 tablespoon oil
butter, honey, or syrup

Put the cornmeal, salt, sugar, and butter in a bowl. Add the boiling water and mix thoroughly. Pour into a saucepan and place the pan on a burner set on low heat. For the next 15 to 20 minutes, stir constantly and keep adding enough cream or milk to keep it about the same consistency as mashed potatoes. When done, drop heaping tablespoon–sized lumps on a hot pan or griddle, which has been greased using the oil. Cook until golden brown on each side. Serve with butter, honey, or syrup. Makes about 30 cakes.

· MAPLE SUGAR ON SNOW ·

butter or grease
1 pint maple syrup

snow or crushed ice

Apply butter or grease around the rim of a heavy pot that can hold 3 quarts or more. Bring the maple syrup to a boil. Reduce the heat. Stir constantly with a long-handled wooden spoon. Simmer until the syrup reaches a temperature of 230 degrees on a candy thermometer (about 5 to 10 minutes) or until a tablespoonful of it becomes soft and waxy, like taffy, when dropped on packed snow or crushed ice. Ladle it out in strips over packed snow or crushed ice. Makes 4 to 5 servings.

· SHOOFLY PIE ·

pie pastry, one-crust, in a 9-inch pie pan
For filling:

¾ cup molasses
¾ teaspoon baking soda
½ teaspoon ground cinnamon

pinch of ground ginger
pinch of ground nutmeg
¾ cup boiling water

For crumb mixture:

½ cup shortening or soft butter
1 cup brown sugar

2 cups sifted flour
¼ teaspoon salt

Preheat oven to 350 degrees. Make the pie filling by mixing the molasses, baking soda, and spices in a bowl. Add the boiling water and stir.

To make the crumb mixture, in a separate

bowl, cream the shortening or butter with the brown sugar, flour, and salt. Put two-thirds of this crumb mixture in the empty pie shell. Pour the filling on top, then sprinkle with the remaining crumbs. Bake for about 20 to 30 minutes, or until filling is firm when touched lightly with a wooden spoon. Makes 6 to 8 wedges.

· FRIED APPLE RINGS ·

oil or shortening
tart, firm apples, cored and cut into 1-inch-thick
    slices
brown sugar

Put enough oil or shortening in a frying pan to cover the bottom. Cook the sliced apple rings in hot fat until they are tender. Sprinkle both sides with brown sugar and eat.

· GINGERBREAD ·

½ cup butter
½ cup strong, hot coffee
2 eggs
½ cup sugar
½ cup light molasses
1½ cups flour

2 teaspoons baking
    powder
1 teaspoon ground ginger
¼ teaspoon each ground
    cloves and allspice

Preheat oven to 350 degrees. Melt the butter in the hot coffee. In another bowl, beat together the eggs, sugar, and molasses. Combine this with the butter-coffee mixture. Stir in the flour, baking powder, and spices. Spread the soft batter in a greased and floured 8-inch square pan. Bake for about 25 minutes or until a toothpick placed in the center of the gingerbread comes out clean. Makes about 6 to 8 servings.

· APPLE BROWN BETTY ·

3 cups sliced, peeled
   apples
1½ cups soft bread
   crumbs
½ teaspoon ground
   cinnamon or nutmeg or
   both

½ cup brown sugar
¼ cup melted butter or
   margarine
¾ cup hot water
ice cream or whipped
   cream (optional)

Preheat oven to 350 degrees. In a bowl, mix together the apples, bread crumbs, spices, and brown sugar. Place in a greased 1½-quart baking dish. Mix together the melted butter or margarine and water and pour on top of the fruit mixture. Bake for about 40 minutes or until the apples are soft. Serve plain or top with ice cream or whipped cream. Makes about 4 servings.

· CORN CUSTARD ·

3 eggs
2 cups canned corn, drained
2 tablespoons melted butter

1 cup milk
1 teaspoon sugar
soda cracker crumbs

Preheat oven to 300 degrees. In a bowl, beat the eggs well, then add the corn. Mix in the butter and milk, stirring well. Add the sugar and pour into a buttered 2-quart baking dish. Sprinkle with the cracker crumbs. Bake for about 30 minutes. Makes about 6 servings.

· APPLESAUCE ·

4 apples
⅓ cup water

cinnamon (optional)

Peel the apples and cut them into eight seedless pieces each. Put the apple pieces and water into a pot. Cover the pot with a lid and place over the stove burner on low heat. Cook, stirring from time to time, until soft, about 15 minutes. If the apples seem to be sticking to the pan or burning, add a little more water. Remove the pan from the stove and stir to blend. Use a potato masher or wooden spoon to mash the soft, cooked apples until they are as smooth as you like. Sprinkle with cinnamon if desired. Makes about 4 servings.

BOOKS FOR FURTHER READING

Bailey, Carolyn Sherwin. *Children of the Handicrafts.* New York: Viking, 1935.

Becker, May Lamberton (ed.). *Golden Tales of New England.* New York: Crown, 1985.

Buley, Roscoe Carlyle. *The Old Northwest Pioneer Period, 1815–1840.* Bloomington: University of Indiana Press, 1951.

Casner, Mabel R., et al. *Story of the American Nation.* New York: Harcourt, Brace & World, 1962.

Cox, Sandford C. *Recollections of the Early Settlement of the Wabash Valley.* Lafayette, Ind.: Courier Steam Book and Job Printing House, 1860.

Crèvecoeur, J. Hector St. John. *Sketches of Eighteenth Century America.* New Haven: Yale University Press, 1925.

Dodge, Bertha S. *Tales of Vermont Ways and People.* Harrisburg, Pa.: Stackpole, 1977.

Driggs, Howard R. *The Old West Speaks.* Englewood Cliffs, N.J.: Prentice-Hall, 1956.

Folklore of American Holidays. Detroit: Gale Research, 1987.

Furnas, J. C. *The Americans: A Social History of the United States, 1587–1914.* New York: Putnam's, 1969.

Greene, Stephen. "Sugar Weather in the Green Mountains." *National Geographic,* April 1984.

Hornung, Clarence P. *The Way It Was in the USA: 1850–1890.* New York: Abbeville, 1978.

Ingraham, Leonard W. *An Album of Colonial America.* New York: Franklin Watts, 1969.

Kilpatrick, James. "Harvest Time Is the Best Time." *Southern Living,* October 1981.

La Lavine, Sigmund A. *Handmade in America: The Heritage of Colonial Craftsmen.* New York: Dodd, Mead, 1966.

Lee, Douglas. "The Plain People of Pennsylvania." *National Geographic,* April 1984.

Paysour, Conrad. "Molasses: Syrup Made the Old-Timey Way." *Greensboro News and Record* [N.C.], October 6, 1985.

Rohrbough, Malcolm J. *The Trans-Appalachian Frontier.* New York: Oxford University Press, 1978.

Stewart, George R. *American Ways of Life.* Garden City, N.Y.: Doubleday, 1954.

Tannahill, Reay. *Food in History.* New York: Crown, 1989.

"Tap Those Maple Trees." *Colonial Homes,* January–February 1981.

Tunis, Edwin. *Colonial Living.* Cleveland, Ohio: World, 1957.

———. *Frontier Living.* Cleveland, Ohio: World, 1961.

Unruh, John D. *The Plains Across: Overland Emigrants and the Trans-Mississippi West, 1840–60.* Urbana, Ill.: University of Illinois Press, 1979.

Welch, Linda. "Using What They Had." *Southern Living,* October 1981.

Wells, Rhea. *An American Farm.* Garden City, N.Y.: Doubleday, 1928.

Woodard, Luke. *Pioneer Days.* Indianapolis, n.d., quoted in Roscoe Carlyle Buley, *The Old Northwest Pioneer Period, 1815–1840.*

INDEX